Life Drawings

by

Lesley Walter

ISBN 978-1-877010-52-1

Walleah Press
PO Box 368
North Hobart
Tasmania 7002
Australia

admin@walleahpress.com.au
http://walleahpress.com.au

Cover image: pencil sketch 36 x 57cm by Lesley Walter
Author's photograph, back cover, by Charlotte Walter

Lesley Walter is a widely published Sydney poet whose first collection of poems, *watermelon baby,* was published by Five Islands Press in 2000. She holds a Master of Letters Degree in Australian Literature from the University of Sydney, and was awarded the Dame Leonie Kramer Prize in Australian Poetry for her thesis on the poetry of Kate Llewellyn. She has always had a passion for language and languages, and this has translated most recently into her completing a Diploma in Spanish, as well as a Certificate in English Language Teaching to Adults (CELTA). Amongst other things, she now teaches English to non-native speakers.

In memory of my parents

muslin moon
in a day-time sky —
you're never far from my thoughts

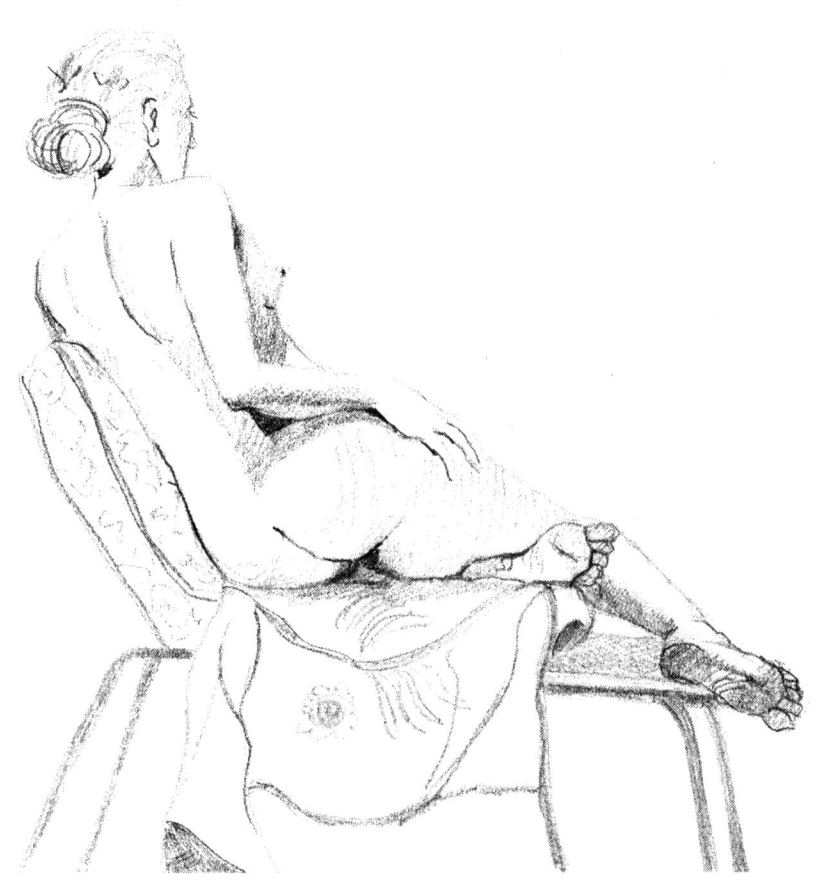

Contents

"Why write?" the sceptics ask,

"and what's more — *poetry?!*"

I *could* say
I write because friends keep giving me notepaper for Christmas,
or because my eyesight's failing and I can make my print as large as I like.
I *could* say
I write because it beats walking around K-Mart when the kids have
    gone to school,
or because it keeps Bic in business, or *me* out of the kitchen.
I *could* say
I write so that I can quote at least one author off by heart,
or because I don't know enough theory to 'make it' as a critic...

But really —
I write to make a mark in empty space.
I write because words and their patternings consume me.
I write because few things bring me a greater sense of satisfaction.
I write because every piece of writing's a surprise, a revelation —
    like the 'paint with water' pictures that enthralled me as a child.
I write as a celebration.
I write so I won't forget.
I write to make something concrete and lasting out of the fleeting,
    the intangible and the ever-changing.
I write in an attempt to wrest something perfect from imperfection,
to harvest a grain of what can't be contained.
I write to make sense in the face of absurdity,
order of incoherence,
art of the everyday.
I write to uncover truths.

I write to lay ghosts to rest.

I write to stay sane.

I write, now, out of fear. That I might never write another poem again.

I write, now, out of gratitude. For each small spark of inspiration.

I write because I believe it's important to express and to share our
humanness.

I write because everyone is like me. I write because no-one is.

I write out of a need to make connections – with parts of myself
that I've lost, repressed, or didn't even know I possessed.

I write to keep myself company.

I write so I don't feel alone.

I write because I believe what every person thinks and feels matters.

I write from a desire to be here for my children when I'm gone.

I write   because   not to do so, now,

would mean existing in some pre-Copernican state –

on a world so flat   I might just as well walk off its edge

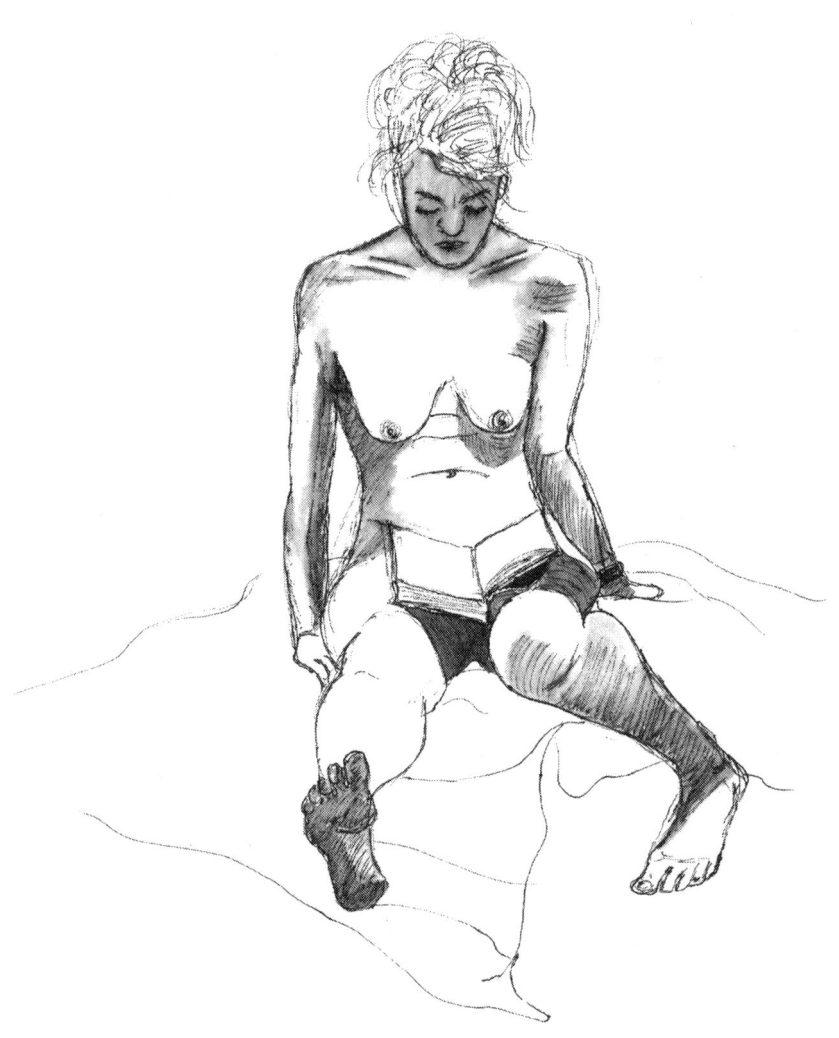

Some day,

strangers will live in my mother's house –
people who aren't even remotely related.
They'll walk in off the porch with their shoes on,
not bothering (when they *know* their soles are clean)
to wipe their feet on the coir mat;
they'll nurse young children on their laps in the living-room,
unconcerned that the extra weight on the chair-legs
might mark the lino tiles;
they'll go to cupboards without always using the knobs,
knowing that unsightly fingerprints can easily be wiped off;
they'll use the dining room – not once a year,
but every time that friends or family visit –
unperturbed that a drink might spill
or a few crumbs fall on the floor;
they'll open windows wide,
leave blinds up
and curtains pushed to the side;
they'll sit on beds after they've been made,
and use cushions as cushions – not as decorations;
they'll hold parties
and invite people who aren't entirely respectable –
who aren't necessarily church-goers
or members of the Bible study group;
they'll wet the glass in the shower recess
and not towel it dry after every use;
they'll indiscriminately use both toilets.

Their children will sit and play boardgames on the floor in the hall
(or even in the loungeroom which is only meant for adults)
and no-one will think
to cover the apricot-coloured carpet with plastic;
they'll reach out to the shiny baubles on the Christmas tree
without being told not to touch;
they'll be permitted to join in
small rituals like tea-drinking,
in recognition that they are people,
rehearsing to be adults one day, themselves;

they'll play chasings on the lawn
and ball games on the back terrace;
they'll be allowed to encourage the neighbour's cat;
they might even *own*   a dog...

Some day,
strangers will turn Mum's house into a real live home –
not knowing she'd have greeted this
tight-lipped with disapproval.

Making toast

My mother is making toast.
She sets the dial at maximum heat,
slots in two slices of bread.

"That setting's way too high," we say,
"unless you want charcoal for breakfast!"
But

"I hate anaemic toast!" she chips,
"I like my toast well-done."
Yet ...

she stands guard,
presses *Cancel* every eight seconds,
sends those still-pale slices down

again and again
and again,   until –
in the end –

her toast is perfect: golden...
"See!" she gloats, "I told you so!
Ex*act*ly the right setting!"

A trip up the river,   together

On the rivercat
    mum can't relax —
        everyone's seat is better than ours.
            Within ten minutes
                we shift three times,
                    but in the end
                        enough is enough.
                            Content with the sun where it is,
                        the scope of our window,
                    the views on our side of the boat
                and the colour of our seats,
        I insist on staying put.
            But mum, nonetheless, moves on.
                From where I sit then
                    five rows back,
                        I watch the top of her head:
                    and in the breeze
                from a now-open doorway,
            her hair unhappily blowing.

Fish and chips   and vinegar

We sit with fish and chips at Botany Bay,
our backs to the winter sun. It's a mid-week afternoon,
the beach, almost deserted. Seagulls bank
and swoop above the strip of sand before us; two
perch on the promenade rail – one, on its single
thin red leg. A few ruffle feathers, squabble
hopefully round our seat, but every time one comes
within our reach, she swings a leg out sharply like
a reflex hammer's hit it, or like some petulant child
giving an unloved cat a kick. I can sense
her satisfaction were her shoe to crack on bone.
She's 83: the world, no more her oyster.

Damn things! she spits.
They ought to keep to the water where they belong!
I toss a scrap of fish. *Don't **feed** the wretched things!*
*Once you feed them they **never** leave you alone!*
She flails her arms wildly, half-rising from her seat.
Ssshhh! Ssshhh! she hisses, as loathe to share
this shoreline with the gulls, as she is
with any other thing that isn't in her likeness.

Everyone I've seen while I'm sitting here's Chinese!
Two Asian women stroll the path below us –
the younger pushing a pram, the elder
hugging a baby to her chest.
You hardly see an Australian any more!

Shoo, shoo, you nuisances!
*It's not **my** fault they've invaded!*
*I told you **not** to feed them!*
At 53, I'm a difficult girl, still bent on flouting her wishes.
*Oh, **there's** one in the **water!** she mocks,*
chuffed at her own cleverness.

I point to a small grey poodle frisking along
the water's edge, reeling itself in and out
on an imaginary line to its owner,
its pink tongue lolling with happiness.
Dogs shouldn't be allowed on beaches!
"But you might recall we took *our* dog to the beach
when we were kids…"
*Oh, I **knew** I'd be **wrong,** she murmurs.*

There's a sudden noisy uprising,
a flapping-and-whirring of wings.
Good riddance! she tosses after them.

But as they leave, one dumps its shit on
my mother's soft white head;

and there's such a mess
of emotions:

her pale bared scalp… my wiping it…

Dogs and cats and daughters

When mum comes to stay these days, it's with a clutch
of plastic bags. Some contain an overflow of clothes; others –
her cereal, a couple of old potatoes, a few stray carrots,
a wedge of overripe melon, the rusted heart of a lettuce.

They're tucked away in the fridge somewhere
or left to clutter benches. And there's always
her packet of biscuits, wound in yet more plastic.
Our small dogs run to meet her, their tails wagging

greetings, their eyes bright with hope. Her response
to them, however, rarely ever changes. "No, go away",
she remonstrates, "I've just washed my hands."
Or when our cat seeks out her lap –

"No, go away. I don't want you on my slacks."
She's rummaging this morning in her suitcase on the floor.
One dog approaches. Sniffs
the swaddled biscuits lying there beside it,

trots on past, indifferent.
Mum lifts the pack and chides thin air –
"Don't touch!" she warns. Her voice is stern.
"There's absolutely nothing for you here."

Circles

Let out the back door
our contrary cat
scales the side fence
and meows at the front.

Let in the front
she struts out the back
scales the side fence
and returns to the front;

like time spent with
my mother now
(the mind's disintegration...)

round and round and
round and round –
our giddying conversation.

Retrospective

Manly Beach 1957

This photo's caught the three of us
squinting into the sun, surf and shore-line
behind us, one side of my mouth hitched up

in an Elvis Presley smile. We're in cotton floral
'cossies' that are shirred across the back,
with bloomer-legs and straps around the neck

that dragged and cruelly pinched when they were wet.
The frill around my neckline's drooped.
One nipple peeps, a small pink rising sun

above its rim. Those costumes didn't dry
from one swim to the next, and the sand trapped
in their gathered legs and crotch chafed

to prickly red our smooth white skin.
White zinc's spread like bandaids on our noses,
on our cheeks. Pale-green plastic swimming caps

snugly mould our heads. Tied beneath the chin,
you could barely pull the knots undone once
the strings were wet. Yellow rubber

surf-o-planes stand propped on end in front –
shark, sword-fish, octopus, stencilled
blue and orange down their length.

These were days of paper cut-out dolls,
of cubby houses, tea-sets, fancy dress,
of kittens dumped like gifts out of the blue

on our back steps. Days we needn't weigh
a parent's love. There was enough.
We pressed unyielding babydolls hard

against our chests, not knowing how
impossible it is, in life, to keep one's children safe.
Our grandad took the snap. He didn't

swim himself. Wore trousers held
with braces to the beach, a tie, black
shoes and socks, a grey felt hat,

a shirt just one shade whiter than his skin.
Nanna sat on a folding canvas seat
in silk dress, stockings, jewelled brooch and beads,

an umbrella opened-out above her head.
And out beyond this small world's frame
lay all those things one never knows   are coming...

Bubble gum

balloom\
like the glossy transparency\
of a beached bluebottle; if left\
too long beyond the tide-line,\
shrivelling, withering,\
becoming dull and\
collapsing in\
upon itself.

As children,\
we would stamp bare-heeled\
on those glassy blue bladders,\
tentatively bold,\
laughing shrilly,\
surprised\
at their resistance underfoot\
before the pop;

shocked\
when they burst\
in clotted strands\
upon the sand,\
or as flimsy films\
of perforated pastel\
in our faces.

Faces

There
are
faces drawn on
*every*thing: not just balloons,
but beads and blocks, and even
now, the pepper grinder. Our
six-year old's creating poems -
she's breathing life into
the lifeless. Her room
resounds with
poetry. I hear
it when I
tidy up... I
place (don't
throw) beads
in their box,
prop teddies tired
against the pillows,
tuck baby dolls snug
into cots, save soft toys
from suffocation. A pale
balloon just hovers, watching,
too shy to start a conversation.
At dinner-time I'm mortified. I
feel I should apologise when I
knock the pepper grinder flying.
I rush, of course, to help it up...
It just lies there, flat on its face.

First fall

She's reassured by *this won't hurt a bit,* then
daddy's finger presses, flicks –
it flies in the air
it falls to the floor.
Those of us present
drop to our knees –
scouring the floorboards assiduously.

In a flurry of excitement
she rushes off
to find the mini porcelain pot
in which to pop her prize:
her first.
Her proud-shy smile reveals a gap –
sorely tender...

I stare
at the miniscule ivory spade
which nestles in my palm.
I strain
to catch its faintly whispered,
slightly lisped farewells.
Then turn.

I study anti-poaching laws
lock the doors
put gauze on the windows
block up the chimney,
in a last desperate bid
to fend off patient
but very determined fairies.

Daughter

We're shopping together
when she suddenly says,
I wonder what my teddy's doing,
left by himself in the car...

I counter, *Probably misbehaving,*
but think, instead, *He's missing you —*
knowing what a morning's like
without her...

Betrayals

Our daughter's room is peopled with things
born of fertile imaginings.

On blocks, balloons, buttons, socks,
are faces drawn in texta pen —

black-lashed eyes, red
mouths forever smiling.

When balloons with names
like Sally and Rose begin to shrink and wither

(their smiles puckering up like old witches' lips),
I'm moved to quietly dispose of them,

choosing a time
when my daughter's not home,

knowing her bent to protect them.
Alone in her room, then,

I stick in a pin
throw the scrap in the bin…

but oh, this uneasy feeling —
as though I've just killed something living.

To my stepdaughter

It was mandatory for me *not* to be at your birth —
(a stipulation of the job description) — what's more,
your father and I only met six-and-a-half years later.
But not all of us grow apples

or know where poison is bought
(and as if I would bother to polish one up
on the remotest chance that you'd eat it!
You *know* I abhor dusting...)

What you may or may not have realised, still,
is that each time I offered you mango
I knew it was simply your favourite...
(Ditto my cooking lasagne, or tacos with hot chilli sauce.)

True, you're not bone of my bone,
and, no, you're not flesh of my flesh
(and we can't pretend that's unimportant...),   but
we *are* bonded by blood —

as though we've slashed our veins
and rubbed our wrists together:
your genes and mine, mingled,
in your father's — and my — daughters.

Three into two...

It comforts me to think
that my girls will have
each other when I'm gone,

as they had, of course,
through all those years
from *my* birth 'til
the first of *them* was born, but

just as, now,
two only
share a room,

I wonder if,
as three small cells,

one

was in an ovary
on its own...

Beach Walk II

Cave Beach, Jervis Bay, January 2001

Scalloped tiers of sooty shearwater gulls
lie strewn where higher tides have left them beached —
the not-so-strong who failed this last migration.
They're left en masse to rot upon this shore,
while steadfast mates and last year's nests await them.
Heads loll limply back upon skewed necks,
twig-like feet are clenched, drawn in and up;

crabs, or other birds, or perhaps fish,
have hollowed out these once-warm, urgent breasts
and small white bones lie sun-dried and exposed.
We pick our way with care amongst the dead.
The sand we tread is fine and soft and white
but where some recent tide has licked and dried,
it stretches in unbroken sheets like ice —

strange, dry ice that cracks beneath our feet.
We stoop and slice our hands beneath these fragile
plates of sand, contesting as to who
can lift the largest — crisp, unbroken — on her palm.
One daughter thinks to follow dad, who deftly
stamps on small blue sacs of air. They burst
for him, but merely dull and shrink at her

attempts – she's thin on courage when her feet
   are bare. We turn at last, head back to thongs
      and towels. The breeze has picked up sharply from the south
         and lifted wings at right-angles from the sand.
      The beach appears a weird, white, wind-whipped sea,
   spiked with tremulous, dark-grey feather-sails.
While wet shells wink, small beacons, on the shore.

Firstborn: The Word Incarnate

(Noosa Beach, 2002)

1 **B**ehold him, where he frolics on the foreshore under a vast cerulean sky; watched over by the trinity of mother, father and grandfather.

2 Mindful of sharks, blue-ringed octopi and the fatal crown-of-thorns, dad kneels to dig his infant son a pool in which to splash — beyond, as well, the imminent threat of waves. (There's no sign, yet, this child will walk on water…)

3 He sits back. Holds out to the boy in the palm of his hand the glory in a grain of sand; the wonder of a starfish, sea-weed, crab.

4 Mum fills and inverts, fills and inverts, fills and inverts a bucket. Turns out perfect castles that the toddler, squealing, smashes.

5 She smiles; serene. Content to make such slight sacrifice to this small god's hungry pleasure.

6 While granddad sits in sandals and socks; captures the morning on film.

7 Later, in the makeshift shade of the umbrella, mum lays her baby down.

8 This precious child, her firstborn — *(You have filled my heart with greater joy!)* — as perfect as the shell he's garnered from this morning's wondrous harvest — clutched tightly now in his own miraculous fist.

9 She anoints his infant skin; swaddles him in a towel; gathers him into her lap.

10 Come time to leave, dad's loaded up like a donkey, with stroller, umbrella and towels.

11 Then granddad raises the boy up; shoulders him off the beach; while mum ministers in their wake to those small sand-peppered feet.

12 And lo! Grandma's there on the boardwalk! She draws a singlet from her bag, eases it over the child's compliant head.

13 Mum threads one arm through an armhole; dad, one arm through the other; while granddad unfurls the garment, like a small scroll, down his back.

14 They crown the child when he's stroller-bound; wheel him off through the piercing noon-day heat — seemingly dead to the world.

15 I squint into the vast cerulean sky; glimpse the evening star — winking in the distance.

Alphabetical types

the alphabet has its oddball characters —

generically, **l**'s tall and lean
thinks **b** and **d** are fat, unfit,
while *they* belittle **a** in terms of stature

f is in an awful slump
t (with **e** and **a**) gets drunk
h will often only speak in whispers

i and **j** are plagued with spots
x is permanently cross
and **m** is literally twice the trouble **n** is

g has guts, it leads with grit
but in the end, **i** and **n**
will *even* dampen **g**'s enthusiasm

u feels used and cannot see
why **w** can't be double **v**

z is always in a tizz
k, it seems, forever in a pickle

e is closed-
yet **c**, quite open-minded

"mind your **ps** and **qs**", they hear
so **p** and **q** just sit and watch each other

s tacks on
to any group soever

r is easily overlooked
y is thoroughly put out
when **s** defers to **i** and **e** so often

y asks one interminable question

when everything is said and done
o's the one well-rounded one amongst them

a, of course, can get away
but none can, outwrite, outrun any other

pushed into relationships together
it's a wonder they say anything whatsoever…

Simply mind-boggling

My partner's into esoterica –
conducts convoluted research
into highly complex questions,
publishes academic papers
involving problematic processes
internationally.
Yet asked to phone our children's school
(situated locally),
professes that he can't.
Simply says he doesn't know the number...

Tricky turns of phrase

"This shirt needs a button," he drops, bending to the mirror.
His back to her, she chooses not to answer.
"IP?" he queries (that's the name he gives her).
"That's not the proper way to ask." She's suddenly the teacher.

"I *didn't* ask," he boldly owns, cocky, now, on grammar.
"You did!" she contradicts, "I*P?* forced an answer."
"This shirt needs a button please," good student, he corrects.
"Not *quite* right, yet," she coaxes (she can't be any gentler).

"Well, *what* then?" He gives up.
(He won't be pushed much further.) "Could you please
sew a button on this shirt for me?" she tenders.
Reluctantly, he parrots words back to her. But —

'please' requires a 'thank you'…
and, 'for me' implies a debt…
What nifty trick was this, he thinks,
to make a *shirt*'s need somehow seem like *his*?!

With my own petard

He's picking up my tricks of trade
and, so it seems, *I* am learning *his...*

Scraping our plates post-prandially,
I find the tidy full-to-overflowing.

"This bin can go out now," I toss,
(he's sidling past, unseeing).

"A bin can't go out by itself,"
he tosses back quick-smartly —

"Will you take this bin to the garbage please,
don't you mean?,   **Darling?"...**

Sex beyond the grave

"In the *next* life", he projects, "I don't think there'll be any sex."
"You never know your luck," I say, "besides which, in the next life,
you'll share it with *three* wives" (cat among the pigeons? or

Daniel thrown to the lions?), "your options, multiplied threefold –
completely spoilt for choice!" Thinking quietly to myself, "Ah, bliss!
The pressure will be off *me,* then, with A and E for the taking",

(forgetting, for a tick, their later husbands), "for, after decades
spent with me, they'll both seem fresh again." (And as for *my* celestial bliss –
I'm praying there'll be more to read than just The One Good Book...)

So, with wings folded neatly by the bed and halo placed on top
(moonlight for romantic ambience), he might rightly 'know' any or all of us,
find himself transported nightly – if not to seventh heaven as such –

perhaps as far as cloud nine. The aeolian harp may lull him
into thinking, "Wow! Perfection!", yet given the lofty location,
I doubt he'll feel the earth move   ever again.

Economic rationalism   and cats

My husband thinks all animals should be work-horses,
even if they're guinea pigs or rabbits. As a child he never
owned a pet, but I sense, were he to choose one now,
it'd be a husky that could haul the bins the length
of our side-passage, or an elephant to lift and carry bricks.

On further thought, a sheep or goat would minimise
the mowing; a giraffe would lop the tops of trees, could trim
with ease the wisteria growing rampant on our trellis.
A cow, of course, could give the family milk, while a can
of cat-food's "simply money wasted". "Why on earth

would anyone want a *cat?*" he daily wonders. "Who do *cats*
look after but themselves?" And yet, our own's a priceless
oeuvre d'art around our home, gracing every graceless chair
she deigns to sit upon. She curls, a living sculpture, on our
doona – each pose of hers so charming yet so wholly

uncontrived, I'm moved to snatch a pad and pen and
sketch her. Life-models earn up to $30 an hour,   *so* –
though I doubt my husband will admit it, Thecat
in fact   does work. She might be soft (and sleep a lot),
but still,   she's well and truly earned her keep.

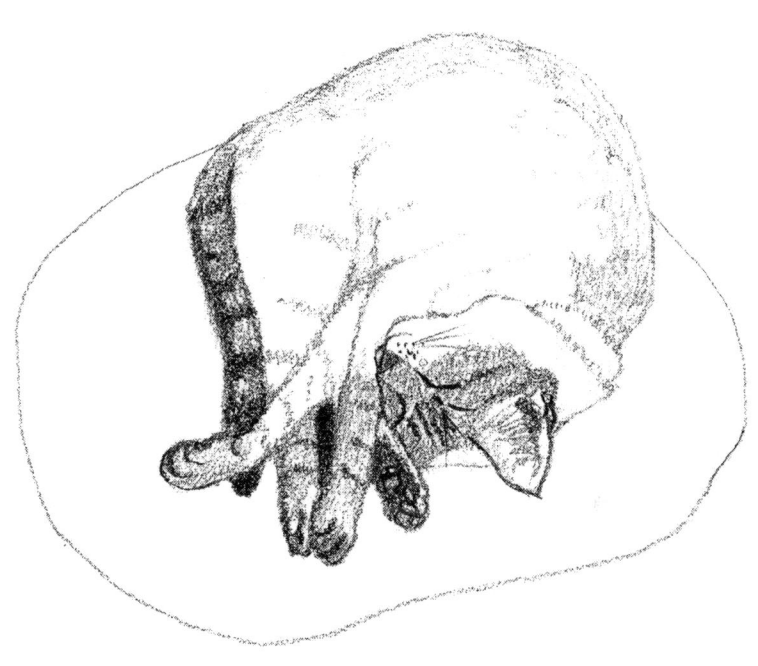

And dogs...

But wait! He's finally bowed to family pressure —
we've bought two(!) pups (X Pekingese/Chihuahua...),
and while I sense they won't drag out the garbage,
at 4k each, they're bound to pull their weight.

Two ways of looking at the universe

Speaking to a group of fledgling writers,
I urge them, *Shoot for the moon.*
Even if you miss it, you will land among the stars.[1]

Inspired by this thought myself, I repeat it
to my husband over breakfast.

That's bullshit! he retorts.
It shows an appalling lack of understanding of the universe!
If you miss the moon,
you'll simply hit the sun and burn to death,
or failing that, just fall into an abyss!

Yet *he's* inspired, now! – grabs pen and paper,
draws earth and moon (two tiny dots of biro) close together,
the sun, a larger orb, he stations   way out on the border.

E to M (he scribbles then with illustrative fervour) – *200,000 miles*
E to S – 93,000,000 miles
E to nearest star – several light years away
one light year – 186,000 x 60 x 60 x 24 x 365 miles (x 8 / 5 kilometers)

I neither challenge him nor check his sums for error
(don't even ask what *several's* meant to stand for…),
accepting them for simply what they are –
not metaphors as such, but still
beautiful figures   of speech.

---

[1] Les Brown, cited in *The Artist's Way*, by Julia Cameron, p.123.

walking the dogs —
he and she forever
getting their leads crossed

His Royal Plural in the kitchen

"Have *We* bought new Vegemite yet?" he asks.
"I bought it yesterday," I say.
"And what about honey?"
"Yes," I add.
"So *We*'ve bought that too, have *We*?"

Then bowing to
his realm's occasional duties,
he brings white tea
for him and me
(our shared-each-morning beverage)

decreeing
"You need milk!" –
(and with pointer and royal thumb
pincered together)
"There's only *this much* left".

Cat-wary

I see him interacting with our cat.
Out!   when he finds her on our bed on Sunday mornings;

Move!   when she assumes a spot on the ironing-board in the laundry –
her paws tucked in   slow-blinking in the sun.

He promptly snaps   ***Get off!***   if she springs into his lap,
en route across the lounge to one of **us.**

He doesn't lift her up to shift her sideways down or off –
just barks commands – these have effect enough.

He sneers   *She's just a cat*
(**we** tag her   *Darling   Sweetie   Pet…*)

I marvel at how small-round-soft-and-strokable her head.
Head-size   he quips   *is a measure of intelligence.*

He jeers   *Why aren't you out   catching rats   Youstupidcat?*
She smiles like Mona Lisa from her basket.

I curl for warmth against him in the dark,
recall I've caught no bread or milk for breakfast…

Two of a kind

Winter long I nose out sun —
lap up the puddle spilt on the steps
that face due east, for breakfast;

flee the house's midday chill
with a fold-out chair,
mug of tea and a book;

play cat-and-mouse across the grass
with chinks of warmth
as the sun threads north;

but am forced, by 4, to inch indoors
where, heater on,
I sit and purr —

joined to my cat
from chest to lap
like a veritable Siamese twin.

in the breeze on the rivercat
my bird earrings all-a-flutter

walking to the station –
every cat I speak to
meows good morning

September 1st
wearing new floral leggings –
the spring in my step

breathless spring morning
nothing stirs in our garden
but the cat's tail

spring flowering –
young mothers and their babies
dot the grass

one-year-old reading
her book upside down –
the tender nape of her neck

jewellery box –
my bird earrings caught
in my cat ones

blue-sky day –
the way that little girl skipped
when her mum said *yes*

Give us this day...our daily bread

A young man stops shovelling dirt.
Strides to the kerb, beaming. "What sort of dogs
are those?" he grins. His knocked-skew-whiff cap.

Cross-Pekingese-Chihuahua. He kneels on the grass,
claps his hands, holds them out, inviting.
Tess, small black tadpole, swims her leash

to greet him. "They're beautiful!" he laughs, looking
up. "They've got faces just like mine have!" *So you
have dogs, as well?* I ask. "Yes." *Are they related?*

"Mother and son." *How nice!* I say. "And yours?" *These two
are sisters.* Tess with her legs in the air. This stranger
rubbing her tummy. Such small but welcome offerings

on cold and hungry mornings. It's like walking again
with children. People stop. And talk. You trade
names and ages. You weigh quirks and habits.

This stranger petting your dog feels like an arm
around your shoulder; his gentle, kindly manner,
like a hand upon your head.

Walking the dogs

I love
the one's ungainly gait, the other's
measured trot;
                    the way they stand on small
hind legs to stickybeak in yards;
                                        how
their feathery ears flick up-and-down
with every step;
                    their joyful tails, their nails'
click-click on paths;

                    the way one waggles up
to all and sundry for a pat
                    (while the other –
shy, with doleful eyes – hangs back);
                                        the way
they rise like acrobats in 'hand-stands' when
they squat;
                    and how at 16 Seaview Street
they whimper at the gate – longing to
touch noses with the cat
                    (her name is Twiggy).

I stroll suburban blocks with them for hours.
I love the way they stop
                    and sniff the flowers.

tea warming

(For D and F, on your marriage)

in our blue kitchen
your blue eyes through the steam
from your blue china cup

                                    reaching for the tea-pot
                                    our fingers
                                    unexpectedly touch

in each sip, green slopes
spiked with the tea-pickers'
colourful saris

                        reading each other's tea-leaves:
                        there's sugar in the bottom
                        of our cups

all those ancient maps,
old spice routes… and somehow,
us finding each other…

                                mornings, sharing tea
                                together: night-times, just
                                the one tatami mat

lifting the cup
the chink of your ring against porcelain:
wedding bell

                      in China, a young bride kneels,
                      offering tea to her in-laws
                      in both hands

what need we
of red dates and lotus seeds? –
already amply blessed

                              pouring tea, your bowed head:
                              i bow my own
                              in thanks

Casting off in Tarban Creek

Just metres to our right, feet poised for landing,
a pelican touches down, quiet as a blessing.

We knit the river-water in the still of early morning –
square our blades, then feather,
hear the oars click in their riggers,
take that long   slow   ride up the slide
then push back hard through feet, legs, thighs
to the clean drop,
to the quick catch –
send the puddles, like stitches, away.

I watch the clouds massed
beneath the river's mirror surface,
peer into a clear inverted sky.
A sunken sun breaks blinding
through a gilt-edged bank of cumulus –
I can hardly tell if I'm looking up or down…
We navigate a rivercat's ribbed wake,
needle through chill air. All's morning-drenched.

From Tarban Creek to Hen and Chicken Bay
or round Iron Cove or up the Lane Cove reaches,
we ply the harbour inlets with the colours of our craft,
pattern our own rhythm on the crew-member in front –
square-drop-cleancatch-feather
pulling hands back through together –
knowing that however long the row,
we must purl our way, still, all the way back home.

Growing old, and not

Ten years on, my sister's second-eldest child is,
overnight, the youngest of her offspring.
All three younger siblings have finally outbatted him,
though he never quit the cricket pitch

and he never left the rugby field; nor did he outgrow
his last school uniform. His boyish face looks out
from photographs – the freckled nose, that half-shy grin –
in later shots, with orthodontic braces.

He'd only had the braces off the evening of the accident –
his family never saw his made-new smile.
Trapped inside a car that burst in flames,
the dental records helped identify him…

And I'm thinking of our grandmother (now twenty years deceased),
who'd suffered, as a child, a brother's death. How,
all her long life long, she never stopped remembering
what was lost. How, sometimes unexpectedly she'd say,

"Baby Christie would have been… sixty… seventy… seventy-five today…" –
all the while, still seeing him in baby clothes,
feeling him still tugging at her plaits;
while we, untried, had nudged each other, laughed.

Blessings,

(for Noel Rowe)

You talk of having re-engaged with life –
how you're tuned again to birdsong
in the mornings, how you find yourself
returning to ritualised prayer, how you
couldn't stamp on a cockroach that,
last night, scuttled across your floor.

And friends. You've opened your arms
to them. We drink tea together – you,
reclining on your couch like a buddha
(your quiet wisdom, your measuredness),
me, in the opposite chair. Nothing and
everything has shifted. Our hands cradle

cups; our minds, poems and memories.
We unfold   like wings   with conversation.
I lived and taught where you grew up, and
stranded by floods in Taylor's Arm, pulled
beers for my keep in its landmark pub. In that
same town, a decade on, you were to serve

your last Mass… Crossed paths. Odd
correlations. A deepening of trust.
Regards, and *Cheers,* have given way to
Blessings,… We know when we depart this
life we leave it empty-handed. Where, though,
is it written we need go with empty hearts?

Untitled

(after Carol Ann Duffy's "The Prayer")

For NMR, May 2007

Some days, although we cannot pray, a prayer
will utter itself. Yesterday, you sat
across from me, your breathing strained, your stare
holding in its blue-grey depths the fear that

time is running out. And so it is.
We do not speak of death so much as talk
about our lives. I want to say I'll miss
you when you've gone (but don't, of course). You walk

with effort now; yet rationalise your aches,
your pain, as things you can address. Still,
you talk of travel, what you'll write. You make
brave plans. This fronded jacaranda will,

come November, burst forth mauve and blue.
To live   more miracles… my prayer for you.

In Memoriam

(of Vera Newsom)

There are things almost as cruel as dying young, like
reaching 93 – outliving three of your five children;
eking out your days in an aged care home, reduced

to just a closetful of clothes. There's the waiting, endless
waiting – pressing call buttons to seemingly no avail
(though there's more response when visitors are with you);

there's having this orderly, today, squat face-to-face
to ask you in a too-loud voice, **"What do you think
you'd like for lunch tomorrow?"**, and

while you're trying to weigh the options up
(meat-loaf/chicken-curry; fruit – plain or with ice-cream),
his turning to your visitor instead

to ask about your needs in the third person
(and you, all too aware of shifts in voice).
There's *not* having lost your thoughts; speech; understanding.

There's being rucked into your once-proud clothes, careless
of the way your skirt's caught up, and how the waistband's
clumped under your breasts and how that pinches;

there's having no phone, no library of loved books,
no paintings from your past – nothing to console,
amuse, distract you – just this one room, with its window set

your neck's too stiff to turn to. There's sitting,
so much sitting, slipping sideways
in your chair, until someone thinks to come and prop you up;

there's sensing that your cardigans have gone missing overnight
and fretting as to how you're going to find them;
there's your apology for being 'dim' to an intellect unequal to your own,

your gratefulness – you deem us visitors 'angels'.
There's your having lost the wherewithal to read, now, and to write,
when reading and when writing have defined you, been your life,

with the prospect, still, of reaching 94 (or even more)
in the care of those quite ill-attuned to who or what you are,
to whom poetry means little, if not nothing.

Desert workshop

Our workshop is a *kershef* house in the desert outskirts of Siwa. Six days a week we sit here – 70 unmarried women, embroidering clothes for a foreign designer. We're not paid much, but it's something. Tourists rarely come here – out near the Libyan border – and so, we were surprised, then, when *these* visitors came in. The man looked out of place in a shirt and tie and jacket. And it was all we women could do, *Incha Allah*, **not** to laugh at his ears! Under his cream hat, they stuck out like the Sphinx's! But he didn't seem to notice – our faces being covered. The lady with him looked done in with heat. I think she was his wife, yet he didn't seem to mind a bit that she talked to the men in their company. She was fumbling with a parasol, the likes of which we'd never seen before! White lace! Out here?! But of course, we didn't stare. Women that we are, we kept our eyes lowered. *Her* eyes, on the other hand, were covered by dark glasses. Strange that these women cover their *eyes*, yet leave their limbs uncovered… She dropped onto our cushions, and squeezing between Zeinab and me, started to teach us the names of things we already know in Berber. It was too amusing for words, but she didn't seem to notice. She kept pointing to the denim in our hands, insisting "jeans" "jeans" over and over. Then she took hold of our cotton reels, intoning "silk" "silk" like a mantra. We couldn't say "No, you are wrong". It's not our custom, as women, to contradict a stranger. Finally, though, she'd had enough and lurched back onto her feet. I hope she didn't hear us giggling as she left. The couple was given some sheets embroidered with "C & C", then the lady asked to buy some jeans ("so brilliant!" she said) for her daughter. I heard them give their delivery address but I still don't know where they came from. I've never heard of theprinceofwales, and what, *Incha Allah*, is a duchess?

Visiting my sister

My sister lives in Cairo where mayhem runs amok.
Twenty million people... yet no road rules are evident.
Cars are dented wrecks, their tyres, treadless. Unrestrained
children cruise the interiors. When asked if tyres need

undergo inspection, my sister quips, "Bald tyres are fine.
So long as cars have four of them." No traffic lights
and no pedestrian crossings. To cross an eight-lane highway
you must weave between the cars and pray you'll make it.

Prayers are called five times a day. Allah lives
in Egypt. We hurtle past a donkey on a foot-wide
road-divider. People hang from doors of vans, balance
on back bumpers. Some just drive against

oncoming traffic — they can't be bothered going the extra
distance. My brother-in-law's a generous host, proud
of Egypt's glories. He knows his Pharoahs inside out
(we view their mummies under glass) and all the ancient

gods' compelling stories. Giza's Pyramids, Luxor's tombs,
Karnak's, Edfu's amazonic temples. But wonders seemed
to cease back then — four thousand years ago. Egypt: sliding
backward into sand. Yet my brother-in-law's optimism's

boundless. He tells us Egypt's 'under renovation'.
At Luxor International Airport, bold letters state,
"The modern gate to an ancient civilization"...
but 'modern' Egypt seems to sit, do nothing.

Mile upon mile, shanty cities crowd the River Nile —
the sole source of the nation's irrigation. Plastic
clogs its once-lush banks. My sister claims "The Plastic Bag
is the national bird of Egypt". Black and white,

they're snagged on wire fences. Livestock shares
the rooftop space with myriad satellite saucers.
Women are back in *hijab* now, many wear the *niqab*.
They point at my uncovered hair, my floral skirt

free-flowing. *I'm* the alien here, my difference salient.
We photograph each other taking photos of each other.
Yet one small girl approaches, shyly smiles and whispers,
"Welcome". The belly dancers these days are all Russian.

Friends of my sister (she Palestinian, he Egyptian),
having lived for twenty years in California,
have brought their daughters 'home' so they might find
Islamic husbands... There's talk of how the West

is more polluting than the East; of how
the Towers were felled by the Americans...
And everyone haggling for *backsheesh* — even the boy
out tending sheep whose photograph you've taken.

Everywhere it's "Where you from?",
"No charge to look", "I give you good price madam" —
the five pounds quoted for a carriage ride,
250 as soon as you're seated! At Edfu Temple

a man calls to my husband, "Lucky man with two wives, you!"
(we're travelling with our daughter), then "How-Now-
Brown-Cow", taunting us in English. And always,
people sweeping sand — holding back the desert.

And then, these Cities of the Dead constructed amidst
the living, among them my brother-in-law's family tomb
where my sister (once as close as a twin), wound inside
a clean *kafan*, will one day be buried, with strangers.

These days

it isn't safe to move outside your home.
The news each day is full of beatings-up,
of robberies, unmotivated killings —
due no doubt to immigrants and youths,
to drugs and sex, to weird hairdos, punk clothes,
lip- brow- and nose-rings.

She dislikes the world as it is —
its disrespect for coat and tie,
its disregard of hat and glove,
decent values all tossed in —
the world, she says, is mayhem.

She wheels her wayward trolley round the aisles.
Elderly, alone, an easy target...
She encourages no smiles, invites no-one's attention.
Those tots in passing trolleys might be ploys...
Ignore their grins, just get your shopping done
and go. Home to safety. Though heaven knows
you aren't safe anywhere, anymore.
Not with all these break-and-enters,
the rape of innocent women in their kitchens...

She struggles with her trolley up the ramp.
It's every woman for herself now.
No knights in shining armour to the rescue...

She stops;
looks up.
Her stomach drops,
her heart beats fast.

A scruffy lout with long lank hair
in tatty jeans and singlet top
is lurching down the mall's long ramp towards her.
And not another soul in sight...
Her grip on her handbag tightens.
Abreast, she notes his tattooed arms –
the arrowed heart, the gruesome skull and crossbones.
She startles at his sudden voice,
a grin revealing two front teeth are missing.

Here, lemme help ya with that trolley, luv.
Ya look done in. Just take ya time.
I'll push the bugger t' the top.
Just hang on tight there t' ya bag.
Ya never know who's watchin'.

And shrugging off her brave attempt at thanks –
No worries, luv, no worries in the world...

It not only the language –

there nothing
I want say to him no more. He force
his self on me again last night. His hairy
belly. His animal breath. His noisy animal
grunting. Every day and every night,
the same. His prickle hair. His thick red neck.
His ears. He wedge against me now so hard
I feel I going to scream. He lean so heavy
on me. He swallow up my space. Once
he wink at mates, call me his missus.
I feel special, wanted. But sometime now
I just you asian cunt you fucking bitch.   But still,

my boy bring joy. He stand here in my lap,
his little nose press up against the glass,
his baby hair stand out around his head.
He point and squeal at everything we pass.
He clever child. Learn fast. I proud
to have this son. Want be best mother.
But sad his baby smell it somehow gone.
And now his neck more thicker. Bit more redder.
And some days when he tired and cross,
he make his baby hands in fists and hit me.
It not hurt. He still too small. What hurt
is when my husband see, he laugh…

Hyphenated Lives

Chang and Eng Bunker, 1811-1874

I. Beginnings: Melange, Siam

I cannot turn my back on my brother —
we're fused in front, made to face each other,
can turn our heads only so far. Chang.
Forever in the corner of my eye. We live so close,
our urine often splashes on the other's feet
or slippers. We don't know what it is
to be alone. Pregnant women skirt us
but our mother says she's blessed. We're as nimble
and as quick on our feet as any other, as lithe
in the Mekong as the fish our father catches,
are wont to row his boat for him —
our arms and legs are strong.

II. The Road Show

We're Captain Coffin's "Siamese Double Boys".
People flock to see us. The freckled ones
with funny eyes and frizzy hair *ooh* at our back-flips,
aah at our battledore. We fly across the ground
like the small cork ball with feathers that we chase
for their entertainment. But later, so many questions!
Yet, what of their own strangeness? We would not trade
our band of skin for such hairy limbs and faces.

III. Experiments

Doctors are fascinated – they wonder if
we're really one; not two. They tickle Eng.
I laugh. They prod me in the dead of night.
It is Eng who wakes. They feed me asparagus –
are confounded when Eng's urine doesn't smell.
So, we run our *own* little experiments...
Only Eng buys a ticket. And who can lawfully
throw him off a train because his brother doesn't?!

IV. Turning Point

Yet since our dual marriage, we try to turn
aside as best we can. But I sense my brother's
hand upon her sex, I hear their bliss; am rocked
by them as though upon a ship. I cannot brace myself
against the tempest – I cannot calm the pounding
of my heart, nor slow or quiet the quickening
of my breath. The darkness that envelops us
is nothing. I'll sometimes slip a hand beneath
the sheet and come, as one, with them. At other
times I wake, my trousers wet. I cannot turn
my back on my brother. I cannot turn my back
upon this woman in our bed. But each morning,
we sip tea together from fine blue china cups.

V. Secrets

At first, I was shy. When my husband's brother spoke,
I kept my eyes lowered. But I cannot tell the man
I married secrets, without his brother hearing them as well.
They wend their way into his brother's ear, carried via
the blood across shared flesh. I am wedded, now, to both.
But still, it is my husband's seed trickling down
the inside of my leg. Or is it?

VI. Sisters

We, too, are tied by blood, though not by flesh.
Our bodies spin full circle, separate. Once,
we kept no secrets from each other; but now
I dare not tell her how her husband cups my breasts,
how tenderly he mouths them in the dark.
My brother's hands are deft, the intrigue sweet.
I pity women bedded by one man.

VII. The Allure

Her skin smells of sandalwood, her hair,
of temple flowers. I brush her lips with mine
as she lies slumped across his chest. Her breath's
like clouds of lemongrass and fresh-cut coriander.
I dream again my past; smell again my mother...
Brother's wife, wife's sister – sister-in-law
twice over. Surely, then, as near to me as wife.

VIII. Questions

We do not walk abroad, now, very often.
People turn to look. Not only children point.
It isn't hard to know what they are thinking.
Our cat's tail, too, is a curling question mark.
It asks us who belongs to whom.
We are no longer sure. And does it matter?

IX. The Thin Edge

I do not have my husband's ear. Always,
his brother has it. Though even they are come
to blows, what with Chang's penchant for whisky
and Eng's for late-night poker! But they nested
in their mother's womb together; limbs entwined,
breast to breast; pressing ever closer to each other.
And flesh links them, still, like a broad umbilicus.
I thought through carrying children I would better
understand the bond they share. Bone of my bone...
flesh of my flesh...But no! Every child I grow
is separate. And my sister and I don't speak now –
except for our bickering. Today, she turned her back
on me and simply walked away. It was that easy...
For us...

X. Endings: North Carolina

I'm pinned here in the dark, chilled by his stillness –
can just slip one foot off the edge of the mattress.
I touch the floor's coolness – so different from the marble-cold
of him. I sweat; am faint with effort; can barely muster
strength to rouse my son. He goes rushing
through the house sobbing, *Uncle Chang is dead!*
Already I feel numbness in my toes and in my fingers,
my son's voice sounding like the death knell that it is.

Although this sequence is based on documented fact, the nature of the
marital relationship/s is largely imagined. In terms of paternity, Eng
Bunker and Sarah Ann Yates are documented to have produced 11 children
together; Chang Bunker and Adelaide Yates, ten.

Cold comfort

Pregnancy and birth –
like the togetherness
then the sever
ance of Siamese twins.

Such overwhelming joy
and yet, strangely subtle pain –
those symbiotic bonds
of cord-and-flesh-and-blood-warmth
gone...

Trumpeting twins' separation,
headlines in a paper blazoned –

*Twins sleep
in separate cots
for first time!*

Like public rejoicing
when marriages move
into single beds...

Setting the table...

she remembers how
they used to nest like spoons in bed together —
curves fitting snugly into hollows,   but

now they rest like knife and fork instead —
jutting angles, unyielding edges;   and

knives and forks don't *talk* enough, she muses,
except to offer snippets, barbed or cutting,   and

though they pull together, need each other,   they
may not turn and say "I love you"   ever...

'Til death do them part

Twenty-plus years on, the fabric itself holds. In places
still, is strong. Woven from their interlocking lives —
births, shared joys and sorrows, loved-ones' deaths —
family, friends, become the binding threads (and it's
childrens' fingers that have tied the tightest knots).
He's not given to inspecting things too closely; but
she *is*. She knows there are a number of loose ends:
thinks, to pull on one, the whole could come undone...
(the weave, in parts, too tenuous for comfort). She's
saddened, too, by the way the colour's faded (though,
that, as well, he claims not to have noticed). Every day
they fold this cloth of promise, taking hold of two worn
corners each. They face each other, step two paces
forward, and as they bring their edges up and in, their
feet might meet, their fingers press together. All day
long as they go their separate ways, it holds a shape
in a corner of their home. And sometimes still, on the
coldest nights, it keeps them feeling very nearly warm.

autumn leaves —
it's time to stop
colouring my hair

alone at dusk
watching lorikeets roost
pair by pair by pair

in sleep he murmurs
a woman's name
nothing like my own

my daughter's menarche —
a small unrealised grandchild
bleeds to death

coming home after dark —
moonlight
on the white piano

on the beach,
marriage wedged between us,
we watch lovers kiss

bush walk —
a fallen log reminds me
I'm not young

another summer gone
and my hair, too,
the colour of rain

Peace, Hope and Love

Three
small wooden
figurines, initially
Christmas decorations,
graced the ledge by our
front door for years.
It seemed fitting
when I packed
the tree
away one year
to leave them there, to
welcome friends and family.
But some time back, Peace plummeted
to the tiled verandah floor, splintering beyond repair,
though Hope and Love continued to stand firm, small sentries
by our door. Yesterday, however, Hope took a tumble when
I brushed her with my elbow. Our youngest daughter, with
me at the time, laughed her sunny laugh, though our eldest
claims she's not displeased to live, now, out of home.
She wouldn't want to stay, she says,
in a peaceless house that's hopeless.
So for now, Love stands alone,
tucked well into her corner to
preclude another accident.
Sometimes, though, winds
gust through the security
grille, and swirl around
the verandah's glassed-in space. We
have to trust (now without hope)
she'll stand up to the elements.

Beach Walk III

Wombarra, February 2009

The scope's too vast, but still, you make a start —
how the seagulls breast down on the sand
into the wind, some with head tucked backward

beak-in-wing; how the leonine cliffs
thrust rugged paws into the surf and waves
thud in against them, hurtling spume. How

tidelines of sea-litter lace the foreshore's
length: clumps of kelp, unstrung amber
beads, and floats of stranded bluebottles —

the blue leached out, the bladders, pearly white.
It all seems too unwriteable to write
and yet, words wash from somewhere as you walk.

The sand is soft and yielding underfoot,
the pounding surf a rhythm in your head.
Gazing south, the coastline's smudged with mist

(there's so much we can't see, or know, or speak),
but birds, sea, air, have given rise to thought:
how his eyes don't hold yours when you talk.

Imprints

(for Dad)

Dining at Surjits,
the saffron rice, the colour
of your skin.

Hospital flowers —
bruises bloom
on your limbs.

You can't recall your
haemorrhage. *I* can't forget
your eyes after it.

Your abdomen, pregnant
with cancer, its popped-out
umbilicus.

Remember when you
fell, playing Boules? How we laughed?
That time, you got up.

Eyes flicker open.
You say "thank you" when I kiss
you on the forehead.

Life support —
your hands hooked into
ours.

I write, *the late Keith Ritchie,*
yet you were always
so punctual…

Country Drive

For Dad

Paddocks roll on past – grey sheep on the distant hills
indistinguishable from rocks. Closer to the road,
young white lambs on guy-rope legs
conjure up a landscape from my childhood,
when I'd squat with friends or sisters for long hours on our carpet
playing with a farm-set made of lead. It had once been yours –
suburban lad dreaming open spaces.
I see the long thin wooden blocks for laying out the pastures,
the upright cross-runged gates, the feeding trough for pigs,
the Friesian cows whose black had dulled, whose white looked
    slightly jaundiced.
I see the border-collie dogs in different herding postures,
trees with widespread canopies for sheep to shelter under,
chestnut horses, spindly foals, and a farmer in brown breeches.
And suddenly I remember, too, a calf without its head,
and several cows with snapped-off legs that we'd prop against the fences.
(In those days, maimed or broken things were seldom thrown away –
you'd 'make do', treat the damaged as still precious.)
Some sheep lay, their legs tucked in and under. Others permanently
    grazed.
One piece was of twin lambs lying butted up together;
but my favourite was the tiniest lamb, unsteady on its legs,
that would wobble – like I see one wobble now – and topple over.

Question

Nothing prepares you for the nothingness of death –
only grams, the difference,
yet the weight   like a burden.

My father alive – less than one ounce heavier
than my father dead.
Tell me,   is this all the soul weighs?

His shoes and socks

My father walked with his feet at 10-to-2
like *his* father did
and as I tend to do.

Now my father's passed away
my husband wears the shoes of his that fitted –
the black lace-ups, the Blundstone boots,

the hapless golf pair, bought pre-diagnosis.
I'm struck to find them empty by a chair
or see them worn, now, toes pointing forwards...

I sometimes don a pair of dad's old socks,
draw comfort from my treading
in his footsteps.

Leave-taking

(for Dad)

The day we scattered your ashes, Dad, a light breeze blew,
and cloud-puffs hung like greetings in the sky.
I dispensed my share from your own childhood cup,
the last of what remained of you slipping
past its rim to meet with earth. The breeze
caught my first fingersful, and then
the rest from a sweep of arm, tossed wrist.
You were scarves of dust, floating in warm air.

I sensed your hands on the length of chain that tethered
each familiar gate I opened;   and
in the long-worn tread-marks across paddocks,
I saw you at the wheel of the orange ute,
right elbow resting on the window-ledge,
your inside arm extended in our faces,
pointing out new calves, crops, mended fences.
The hayshed's still the one you built

but the timber cattle-yards have been replaced.
The trees have all grown taller in the sixteen
or so years since we moved on. And the grove
below the house… I saw you in its welcoming
shade, striding in your overalls
and hat down that well-trod track from house to yards to shed,
the dam you drilled – the ducks still – on the right.
The house is painted green – it's been extended –

the shrubs around it, filled-out, new ones planted.
(The house cannot be seen, now, from the road…)
It felt easier, having brought you back to rest here,
to find the place still so carefully tended.
(*You* couldn't leave a stone or log unturned.)
You used to say, "Just throw my ashes on the back
paddock at Crookwell!", but since your death, I've gnawed
at your bravado… *Was* it, in the end, what you intended?

I'd been fretting at the thought of you being left
behind, alone – the region's bitter frosts…
you, chill and desolate. But the day we scattered your ashes, Dad,
the sun shone, and such a light breeze blew
and small white clouds were company up above.
We chose a slope, auspiciously mown, with a favoured
view, and it seemed so right to leave you there,
to give you back to the land you'd worked and loved.

What's erasable, what's not

My mother is cross
at the scuff on the wall in the hallway,
left by 'those careless ambulancemen'

as they stretchered
my father out of their home
after his violent haemorrhage.

She concedes nonetheless –
"Thankfully, there was almost no blood
on the carpet."

One day

I fantasise that, one day, years from now,
when strangers are living in my mother's house,
I'll knock on the door.
I'll say, "This was once my mother's house.
I was passing by. Thought I'd stop."
They'll welcome me in shoes-and-all,
with my daughters, *their* babies,
maybe even a toddler(!) in tow…

Stepping over the threshold,
I'll hardly recognise the carpet,
so odd will it look without plastic.
We'll chat for a while in the kitchen or garden,
then later, retire to the loungeroom, for I hear them insist,
"There's more space in here, love, with the children.
And *please*, don't you worry! Everywhere's child-friendly.
We've got grandkids too, you know. Aren't they just so precious?!"

We'll eat crumbly cake off hand-held plates
("Don't mind the crumbs – they'll easily vacuum up")
and drink from fine bone china cups.
When I remonstrate they'll simply laugh,
"You can't take anything *with* you!"
I'll feel so comfortable
I'll want to kick my shoes off, tuck my feet up.
But I won't, of course, out of habit.

I'll tell them how nice the place feels. They'll say,
"But it was in such great shape when we bought it!
As though it had never been lived in!
Your folks must have been very fastidious."
There'll be no question of my coming again
(and how strange that will seem on my leaving…),
but, even so, on that day in my mother's house
I'll have been made to feel just like family.

Chinese restaurants and take-aways

I.

Two days before dad went into a coma
we had lunch together
in a Chinese restaurant in Enfield.
He'd only just come from his specialist –
had been told he'd be with us for Christmas.
That was November the 7th,
it was the last proper meal he ate –
san choy bow, prawn omelet,
salt and pepper prawns, steamed rice.

And raw chilli!
My eyes sprang with water, but
Dad's began to twinkle!
He skewered a fat red sliver,
swallowed it, playful, brazen.
"Nothing can kill *me!*" he tempted fate.
Then popped his eyes, seized the jug of water,
made as though to gulp the whole jug straight!
How we laughed (once he had recovered…).

That night, dad collapsed. He never stood again.
He passed away, grimly, four weeks later.

II.

The day my father died,
my mother didn't want us
in her home. (In case we dirtied
her oven. In case we turned on her stove.)
In *her* view —

"How bloody rid-**i**-culous!"
Why was my eldest sister,
advised of our father's passing,
driving down from Canowindra
to impose on our mother for dinner!?

"She needs to grieve with us," I said,
"She needs to be with her family."

"She has her *own* family!" mum snapped back.
"She doesn't have to come here!
Well, *I'm* not preparing a meal for them!
We'll book at the Chinese restaurant."

"We're not eating out when dad's just died!
I'll buy chickens," I said, "toss a salad."

"This is *my* house," my mother warned.
"You do as I say or get out!"

I sensed the day my father died
I also lost my mother.

III.

For the disposal of my father's ashes,
my mother spent the night before
pouring them from their collection urn
into four take-away containers,

then spooning them equal measure.
"One for each of us," she explained
(stressing her sense of fairness),
"Everyone with the same share."

So we drove dad's ashes to their resting place
in Chinese carry-out containers,
stacked one on top of the other
in a bag in the boot of the car...

Bearing witness

There's a floral sofa in my mother's house
you're not supposed to sit on.
It's set against a wall behind the other lounges,
its corners plump with cushions, its purpose, ornamental.

There are thick soft towels in the linen press
that have never ever been used.
According to mum, in his last months
my father "bled over everything" –
was allotted, then, only worn-ragged ones.
I can still hear her complaining,
"I can't stand it. It's such a nuisance."

There's years-old linen on the beds,
because "washing *new* sheets will only make them fade".
There are two full dinner sets in the sideboard,
yet visiting, we're given to use
odd plates and bowls and mismatched cups,
chipped now, from my childhood.
The mugs that mum considers best are kept
exclusively for guests from church –
the men, though, not the women –
and seemingly not daughters.

Rolled carpets stand like sentinels in corners.
Purchased with "the very spot in mind" for them to go,
they're too good to put down.
"Thoughtless people in black-soled shoes think nothing
of putting their feet on them."

In pride of place in the entrance hall,
there's the 1960s' shag-pile mat instead —
diamond-patterned, green-and-white-and-black —
favoured by the long-haired (long dead) dog we had
when I was growing up.
Other offcut carpet squares
(the sort you slide beneath your feet in cars)
are placed at various trafficked spots mum fears
will wear unduly.

But what cut deep
were the faded threadbare sheets I helped her wash
when bloodied from my father's fatal haemorrhage:
for the last night dad spent in their bed,
he'd been reduced, I saw, to sleep so meanly.

Now is the winter of her discontent

And all the clouds that low'r'd upon her house
In the deep bosom of my mother buried.

Mum complains about the dirt on the paving
in her courtyard, of the dust along the outside edge
of her wire-screen door. Her cleaning
lady's hopeless *(Big Fat Thing!)* – she really

should get rid of her. She's displeased
with the blossom trees along the side of her house –
how they've grown too big. (Ditto the robinia
along the neighbour's fence.) Once

these were embraced for the privacy they
afforded. Now mum claims they make her place
unsafe. *Nobody can see if someone's*
peering in my windows! She denounces

Madam two doors up, who's taken it
upon herself to keep the water up
to a common bed of snapdragons
between mum's home and her own. While mum concedes

these pretty blooms would perish, left untended,
still she persists: *It's like the woman's*
*cheek! How **dare** she water someone else's*
*flowers! You'd never see **me** doing it!*

At 85, mum's hands

Mum stiffens when I take her arm.
I can do it, she sniffs with scorn,
I manage perfectly well on my own.

Just look at that fat boy!
she'll blurt in other people's presence,   or
Look at that old girl's hair over there!   or

That woman's skirt is rid-i-culous!,
then turn to me, *Well,* **isn't** *it?!*
She won't abide my silence

yet she bristles at dissent, huffs,
I'll go home. We don't agree
on **anything.** She'd like to

slap that hussey's face,
send all those boat people packing,
push that-rat-Kim-Beazley off a cliff,

(John Howard is such a gentleman) —
clutching what she knows and likes,
sacred, to her chest.

But with ring- and little fingers poised
like small pink wings for flight,
mum lifts, I note, a glass

these days
with both hands to her lips,
with bird-hands, sips

then lowers it. And I see
how she's part child again – in need
of my thin patience.

Just borrowing

As well as jam, honey and butter pats (some of them half-used, peeled back), and coffee and sugar sachets swept up from the breakfast table, mum has taken to collecting others' spectacles. Across the table, she looks at me through glasses not her own. The right arm's bent and broken (they sit at a funny angle) and the right lens, wholly missing. When I point this out, she tells me to "stop fussing". "But we've only just had glasses made to correct your double vision..." She shuts me down: "I can see just fine!"

In her room, I search her drawers, uncover yet *more* squirreled ones! But she doesn't want to hand them in. "It's always good," she's adamant, "to keep a spare pair handy".

She has Marge Carroll's nightie and Roma Goodall's cardigan (their names in felt-pen, printed in the necks), and today, two watches swim around her wrist...

Mum hides her *own* belongings so no-one else can take them. She doesn't remember she's hidden them, hence hasn't a clue where to find them. It's always – "Those wretches have taken them". She's ripped holes in her bedroom curtains and threaded her underclothes through them. She knots these closed "so no-one can see in" (even though she's one floor up, with views to a courtyard and fountain). "Bloody buggers!" she constantly seethes, "*I* would never steal *any*thing!"

visiting mum
in the aged care home –
the sorry back
of her sad white head
simply sitting waiting

nursing home resident
tenderly cradling
her baby doll –
if only mum could find
such solace in my visits

Dislocation

These white walls, these white sheets, these white
hospital blankets. Her white hair on the white
pillow, the whites of her rheumy eyes. She stares
ahead at the elderly woman in the bed directly
opposite. The woman is asleep, her head
collapsed into a bony shoulder, her chin

sunk behind the paper bib a nurse
has tied around her neck for dinner (the food
now long untouched on the mobile tray
beside her). Mum stares, but barely registers, her mind
as one with the blanked-out space around her. Her fretful
hands (and still fine dainty fingers) worry

at the sheet and blanket edges, pleating
them together as she purposefully
did the fabrics she once sewed into our
childhood's gathered skirts and our dolls'
matching dresses. "What are you looking for, mum?"
I ask. "Paragraphs...   Salt..."   she thinly

murmurs. Night has fallen outside. Through
the darkened windows, I see coloured lights
reflected in Brays Bay, cars' headlamps
threading across Ryde Bridge; think:
all those people out there, life-enmeshed,
believing, still, they know where they are heading

The photograph

My face has slipped
behind the mount of the photo frame
in the corner of our bedroom.

I'm sitting in a high-backed, wicker chair,
my then-dark hair drawn softly up and back
in the way I used to wear it.

But without quite noticing when,
I've come unstuck. Fallen down
behind the inner mounting.

I've looked at this for weeks
and yet, done nothing –
knowing to recover what's gone missing

means more than just a lift and paste
of that lithe young neck,
that smooth-skinned smiling face...

Getting a life

I'm excited at the prospect of
visiting my kids in their own homes.
I can't wait to saunter in and drop

my stuff in the hall. After a quick "hello",
I'll plomp down in the loungeroom with 'the box',
stretch out with my feet up on the couch,

hang on for dear life to the remote
and watch my favourite show 'til dinner's cooked.
I'll leave my oft-washed hair to clog the drain,

the soap on the shower-floor,
the empty toilet roll blissfully in place.
I'll fail to note *two* toothpaste tubes –

both mangled and half-used –
and blithely set about opening a third one.
Whenever I shower first,

I'll leave the shower cap
scrunched up cold and wet inside and out.
I'll spread my bread for ease without a plate,

leave the crumbs to decorate the bench
(and feed the ants), the Vegemite and honey
without lids, the butter and the jam

out of the fridge. If I spill some milk,
I'll mop it up of course,
then drape the cloth, unrinsed, across the tap.

I'll leave the dishwasher,
cycle done, still stacked,
my breakfast dishes resting in the sink,

and while they vacuum, mop, cook, tidy, shop,
I'll facebook friends and surf the internet.
By then, I'll be too tired to walk the dogs...

And the washing they've hung out?
I'll judge it better rinsed and rinsed again
than ever *I* should rescue it from rain...

If they complain, get angry, seem put out,
I'll simply parrot back their own advice –
I'll tell them not to fuss; to 'get a life'.

Needlework

What did the boys in 3rd grade do while we
took sewing classes? Schoolgirls in the '50s,
bent over huckerback; small fingers plying

needles under cotton filament bridges,
pulling through embroidery thread (how
I loved the colours!), in-and-out in running

stitch – patterning lines and crosses. And what
became of all those handkerchief holders? Progressing
next to gathered skirts – how many thousand

stitches? Every one hand-sewn, minute,
and all of them near-perfect: blind, hem,
blanket, cross, straight stitch, zig-zag, slip;

tacking, catchstitch, herringbone; buttonhole,
top and back. And all our seams were French
seams, too – we weren't allowed frayed edges. I peer

now at the clumsy scar that's pinked down my
right breast, the endstitch pulled a bit too tight,
this puckering of flesh. I run two fingers

down its length and register a ridge,
hard and lumpy underneath – a seam
not rolled, unpressed (the surgeon, male

and fortyish, and very well-reputed). So what
did all the boys do then, while we took sewing
lessons? Woodwork? Dig the garden? Standing

at the mirror, now, I cannot help
but wonder   if a woman would have slit smooth flesh
and stitched the raw-cut edges quite like this...

dromedary vase –
centuries old –
what woman
first set flowers here?
her butterfly-light hands

And still, this yearning...

My friend and I are at a similar stage in life —
our children semi-grown;
in paid, part-time work;
consumed by interests long-subsumed, fulfilling and enriching.

But today, we meet serendipitously
in *Pets World* at our local shopping mall —
surprising each other by the baby animal cages, where,
faces pressed to wire-mesh, we're both held

captivated by pudgy puppies'
soft pink underbellies, their tiny brush-tipped penises,
by kittens' sweet unblinking eyes, their pleading faces, plaintive cries —
longing for the touch of fur or flesh —

alive again to eager mouths teasing toy or breast;
the pawing of small hands;
round, downy heads, scented, warm from sleep,
snug against the palm, cupped to nose   mouth   cheek...

Hardly so surprising, then, to meet here, hip-to-hip —
hands straining hold of shopping bags — full-plenty —
arms aching with the weight
of being empty.

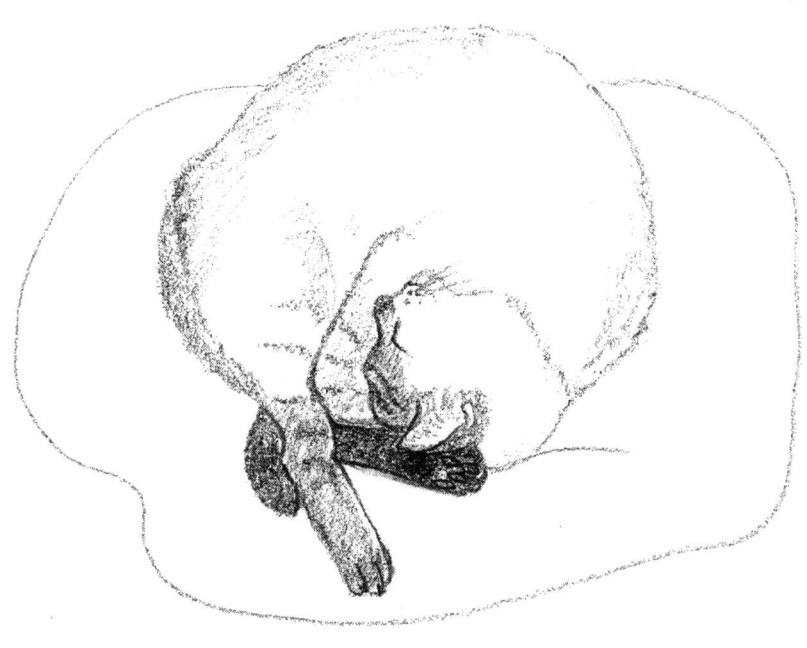

Labours of love

Right now, across this continent, my stepdaughter's
giving birth, coaxing her first-conceived from caul
to light; while I sit with mine, who's ill and feverish,
through long, pain-filled hours in RPA:
the ward where she was born, across the street.

It's two days post this daughter's twenty-first.
She rests as best she can across two seats (there
are no beds), her head weighing heavy in my lap.
Her fine damp hair, her flushed pink cheek...
How memory stirs. I count her toes, her fingers.

Goi cuon

For Charlie

Swaddled in a fine white muslin wrap,
he's a steamed rice-paper roll, his little arms
and legs – pale shrimps, pink vegetables, through the cloth.
And the roll itself is quaintly carrot-shaped.
For, bound like this, his shoulders don't exist.
His torso slopes from tapered neck and chest
to widen and round out at waist and hips
(his feet and knees, a newborn's, still drawn up).
I slide my hands beneath him, lift him up,
press him, tight-wrapped bundle, to my lips.
He's warm and soft and smells just freshly cooked.
My grandson – one week young. So wholly edible…

Acknowledgements

Much has been said about the invisibility of women
past a certain stage in life. And it's not only men
who look through them. It's obvious how children, too,
favour the pretty young teacher. But occasionally,

we are 'seen', as happened today on my walk.
Stopped at the pedestrian lights on the opposite
street corner, was a dad with his baby daughter
(a child some twelve months old, strapped

to her father's back). When the light turned green,
we crossed the road then walked four blocks abreast
(on opposite sides of the street, of course) – the father,
not seeming to notice me at all, yet the child

kept watching everything I did, kept smiling
across the void to me, as though to say
"You're nice". *That* (and the way our cat will choose
my lap) can sometimes, now, suffice.

At the crossing

…clenched in my taut wrists, my hands, the thin
bones of my arms, the certainty that everything
has long been over.

Peter Boyle, *"Missing Words"*

From the driver's seat,
she sees her obstetrician on the crossing –
white coat, stethoscope, a beatific smile on his face
as though he's just witnessed a miracle.

And, probably, he has –
flood of holy waters, sacrificial blood,
the laying of a baby in a manger.

And behind him in that building,
an oyster-woman – shucked of her slippery pearl –
the seed long-fed on its stem
grown now to perfection in the tidal depths of her womb.

She lives again the long hard prising open:
squalling life placed newly in her arms.

But today her hands rest weightless on the wheel,
her lap beneath the steering column, empty.
She feels, again, that painful sense of loss,

like this morning when she chanced upon
a photo of two newly-weds
framed inside a studio's shop-front window:

the laughing bride in lace,
her eyes deflected from the camera lens,
and by her side, the groom —
his gaze turned full on her half-turned cheek,
love's first flush reflected in his face.

chink of blue
on this winter day –
the cat's cobalt collar

a full moon
lights up
his empty side of the bed

fallen magnolia –
I swab my agéd mother's
bruised white stomach

winter sunlight has
shifted off the corner chair
along with the cat

short grey days
and short grey hair –
it's red shoes this winter

passing the cemetery –
just the verge between
me and these graves

winter drizzle,
and the family pets…
bones in our garden

mum's recent death –
now her dressing gown wraps me
in warmth

time spent with my granddaughter –
small moments of Grace

Small comfort

I dreamt of you last night. You'd planted
a garden of pins, point-down in
your carpet — their mini, multi-coloured
heads like a bed of standard roses.

You'd threaded a needle with cotton, then left
it in disuse (the dirndl skirts,
the dolls' dresses you'd sewn for us
as children, all in the far-distant past).

You were using my old sewing basket, the pin-
cushion shaped like a mouse. I sensed a need
to take the lot away — these once
familial, homely things, no longer

innocuous objects. I took you, then,
on some outing, where you fell into
a swimming pool's cold depths, sinking
like a stone. I jumped on in and dragged

you out, chafed you back to life.
It's sad though true we placed you in
that final nursing home...   But, mum,
in my dreams,   I didn't let you drown.

When I leave this life,

I'd like my ashes scattered at 4 Rosemount Avenue
Summer Hill, the home I've lived in longest, the place
I've loved the most. Yes, I love the ocean, but only
for the living... it's trawled by sharks, is wild and dark

at night. Here in the yard it's safe, the light from the house
spilling over the lawn where, every year when they
were young, you mowed our children's ages and initials
in the grass, we sat with friends, our washing flapped

and our pets lazed in the sun. The thrum of distant trains
will still be heard on quiet nights, neighbours' muted
voices; children's squeals from the swimming pool, and dogs
snuffling under the neighbouring fence. I shall not be alone.

The odd cat will wander in and out as is
their wont, the lorikeets pay welcome noisy visits.
The wisteria will burst with lavender blossom every
spring, and the moon rise above our jacaranda.

Afterword

My thanks to the editors of the following publications in which some of these poems have previously appeared: (books) *The Natural Way to Better Birth and Bonding* (eds Naish and Roberts, Random House); (journals) *A Hundred Gourds, Blue Dog, Eucalpyt, Famous Reporter, fourW, FreeXpression, frogpond, Idiom 23, Island, LiNQ, Meanjin, Muse, Paper Wasp, Poetrix, Southerly, Windfall, Yellow Moon;* (anthologies) *Best Australian Poetry 2006, Third Australian Haiku Anthology, Third Yamadera Basho Memorial Museum English Haiku Competition Anthology, Mood Cumulus* (Central Coast Poets Inc.), *Ten Years' Live* (Live Poets' Press), *from the anabranch, Sun and Sleet,* and *Prismatics* (Poets Union Inc.), *Expressions of Faith* (Triumph House, Peterborough UK), *Dreaming the Great Wave, When the Sky Caught Fire* and *This Strange World* (Youngstreet Poets), *Women's Work* (eds Hathorn & Bailey), *100 Tanka by 100 Poets from Australia and New Zealand* (eds Fielden, George & Prime); and (apps) *The Disappearing* (The Red Room Company).

"Hyphenated Lives" won the 2005 Gwen Harwood Poetry Prize, and "Firstborn: The Word Incarnate" won the 2002 Society of Women Writers NSW Inc. Poetry Prize. "Needlework" and "At the crossing" were awarded 2nd Prize in the 2010 and 2012 SWW NSW Inc. Poetry competitions respectively. "Country Drive" was used in the 2007 HSC Practice Examination Paper, NSW English Teachers' Association.

I wish to acknowledge the years of friendship and support from both past and present members of Youngstreet Poets, as well as from members of The Red Dragonflies, a haiku group to which I feel privileged to belong.

I am particularly grateful to Ralph Wessman of Walleah Press for not only accepting to publish these poems, but for welcoming the inclusion of drawings, a vision of mine that was integral to the collection and which he wholeheartedly shared. My gratitude also goes to Jean Kent for her encouragement, and to Brook Emery, Jean Kent and Ron Pretty for their thoughtful back cover comments.

My husband, Terry, deserves special mention. He not only inspires some of my poetry, but also puts up with it appearing in print. I should add that the quirks and foibles outlined in some of these poems are not fully representative of who he is, or what 'we' are. All the poems are life drawings, nonetheless.

Importantly, I pay tribute to the love, care and support I received from my parents over decades. I will be ever grateful for the charmed childhood my sisters and I led. Fond memories far outweigh the sorry legacy of later years which is sketched in some of these poems. The last decade of my mother's life – when her kinder and more generous qualities were largely occluded – was undoubtedly harder, sadder, and more bewildering for her than for those around her. If only for that reason (but for many others, as well…), I wish these poems were different. However, these poems are what they are, because life is what it is.

Printed in Australia
AUOC01n0745110516
275829AU00002B/4/P

9 781877 010521